What's Wrong with the Corporation?
By Robert Villegas

What's Wrong with the Corporation?
By
Robert Villegas

Robertv1989@outlook.com
www.robertvillegas.com

ISBN: 9781695682979
Imprint: Independently published

More books by Robert Villegas
https://amzn.to/2ngaUHb

"Liberty is meaningless if it is only the liberty to agree with those in power." - Ludwig von Mises

The modern mind is beset with a number of cognitive errors that bear upon the purpose of this book. They also bear upon a philosophy which essentially prohibits a free flow of ideas and opinions. This is the philosophy of pragmatism. Yet, few people know they are living under the oppressive nature of pragmatism. Instead, they think they are free to do whatever they want to advance new ideas and challenge the status quo. More importantly, they don't know that their deepest held beliefs are destroying their knowledge of reality and fomenting social failure.

This booklet is part of a larger study about the making of the modern mind. I propose that pragmatism, and its parents in Europe, have negatively impacted man's mind and have restricted human development. In order to understand this, we must understand pragmatism.

Pragmatism is considered to be the first "American" philosophy because of its distinctly American features, its appeal to "what works" and blind leaps of action, its focus on results that have "cash value" and its decidedly false practical mindset. Yet, pragmatism is only "American" if you focus on these derivative concepts rather than its foundational beginnings. The foundational source of pragmatism is European philosophy.

"It is sometimes said that the movement variously called pragmatism, instrumentalism, and radical empiricism is an expression of "Americanism." It is true that most of the leading pragmatists have been Americans, and that pragmatism has had a wider impact in this country than in others. But actually much more than merely local influence went into the development of pragmatism. Hume's empirical analysis, Kant's phenomena (but not his noumena), Hegel's phenomenology and his soft-pedaling of "spirit," the social orientation of the Utilitarians, the positivism of Comte, and Bergson's activism—these and other lines of thought influenced Dewey."[1] (Dewey is one of the founders of pragmatism)

In particular, 'the social orientation of the Utilitarians" has influenced many of today's CEOs, college professors and other Americans. Their calculation of corporate "results" means calculating the views and opinions of society (perception is reality). The pragmatic

---

[1] A History of Western Philosophy by W. T. Jones, Volume IIII, Kant to Wittgenstein and Sartre Page 281

businessperson today walks on both sides of every political fence to avoid displeasing anyone. In fact, being nice and uncontroversial is always counted as the most intelligent way to deal with people among the pragmatists. No businessperson today stands for his right to earn money, express his own opinions and keep the results of his work because that is just too selfish in their view. It ignores the wellbeing of society.

"In Dewey's view, intelligence cannot attain to eternal truths, but, rightly understood and rightly applied, it is capable of dealing effectively with pressing social and political problems...Dewey focused on the actual world and on what "interested" thought can do in it."[2]

"They (the pragmatists) really mean the fact that there are no ethical absolutes. There is no knowledge for certain in ethics any more than there is knowledge for certain in any other field. You have to try and see, you have to experiment, you have to see what works (with people). You have to give up the idea of unyielding, unswerving loyalty to moral principles."[3] (Parentheses mine)

---

[2] Ibid Page 282
[3] The History of Western Philosophy, Kant to the Present by Leonard Peikoff

"Men, instead of being proud of accepting and asserting beliefs and "principles" on the ground of loyalty, will be as ashamed of that procedure as they would now be to confess their assent to a scientific theory out of reverence for Newton or Helmholz or whomever, without regard to evidence.

"If one stops to consider the matter, is there not something strange in the fact that men should consider loyalty to "laws," principles, standards, ideals to be an inherent virtue, accounted unto them for righteousness? It is as if they were making up for some secret sense of weakness by rigidity and intensity of insistent attachment. A moral law, like a law in physics, is not something to swear by and stick to at all hazards; it is a formula of the way to respond when specified conditions present themselves. Its soundness and pertinence are tested by what happens when it is acted upon. Its claim or authority rests finally upon the imperativeness of the situation that has to be dealt with, not upon its own intrinsic nature—as any tool achieves dignity in the measure of needs served by it. The idea that adherence to standards external to experienced objects is the only alternative to confusion and lawlessness was once held in science. But knowledge became steadily progressive when it was abandoned, and clews and tests found within concrete acts and objects were employed. The test of consequences is more exacting than that afforded by fixed general rules. In addition, it secures constant development, for when new acts are tried new results are experienced, while the lauded immutability of eternal ideals and norms is in itself a denial of the possibility of development and improvement."[4]

"When pragmatists do advocate political views of their own, because they have no principles, you cannot get anything too coherent out of them, but the typical pragmatist on the street would be an advocate of a mixed economy. That's the type of system that would fit best with pragmatism politically. Since they have no basic principles in politics, as in any place else, there is no absolute right or wrong political system, they would par excellence be the type that prides itself on being called moderate as opposed to the extremists, you see, who attach themselves rigidly to fixed absolutes, they say all men have absolute rights, or whatever the system happens to be. Particularly today pragmatists would be advocates of the mixed economy because in

[4] The Quest for Certainty: A Study of the Relation of Knowledge and Action by   John   Dewey

politics as in ethics, they are parasitic, they feed off the prevailing value code, they adopt and absorb as they are being brought up the values that are presently extant in the culture and since the prevailing values in America today are a mixture of pro-freedom and pro-collectivism, this is what is present in the mind of the typical pragmatist when he consults his unquestioned values in any given moment, he finds a whole mélange mixed of part pro-freedom and part pro-collectivist values, and therefore, he will oppose absolute individual rights or absolute totalitarianism. There is, I may say a pronounced slant to the left in pragmatists as the country moves further to the left in general, the pragmatists are carried along. The ones I know, I may say, normally call themselves advocates of democracy but they are extraordinarily vague as to what they mean by democracy. I've heard democracy by pragmatists characterized as a system which fosters (mind you, this is a political definition), a system which fosters growth and creativity, shared experience, equality of opportunity. Now, you go and figure what political system would implement that. The one thing you can know for sure is that there will be a pronounced collectivist bias and that will be dictated by their epistemology. If adherence to society is the standard of the truth then society and its welfare will also be the standard of the good; implicitly it has a strong anti-capitalist streak, a kind of woozy socialism which is characteristic of most pragmatists, but it is woozy; one commentator that I've read on pragmatism and is sympathetic said that they are vague on principle because they don't want to commit themselves to some absolute; there is just a very generalized sketch and in particular cases, we try to see whether it works or not. In other words, in politics it has no more specific principles than it does in ethics."[5] (Consider what this means in education)

Pragmatism holds that reality is made by the collective, which, to the pragmatist, makes the views and ideas of people to be very important. To see this more clearly, let's look at the Business Roundtable. The Business Roundtable is a group of 181 CEOs from some of the biggest corporations in the U.S. (including Apple, American Airlines, Accenture, AT&T, Bank of America, Boeing, Comcast and J.P. Morgan Chase and Co.) **Recently, the CEOs of the Business Roundtable decided to change the definition of**

---

[5] The History of Western Philosophy, Kant to the Present by Leonard Peikoff

the "corporation"; a grand gesture whose intent is to change the nature of capitalism itself in the minds of customers, employees and shareholders. Their views are considered important because how they think determines their views of the corporations.

Pragmatists consider themselves to be problem-solvers; but they never solve problems with a sweeping review and sweeping recommendations. They only wait until a problem threatens and rather than changing a whole system, such as capitalism, they merely try to stamp out that singular isolated problem that has arisen. They deal with it then move on to the next problem. This is in keeping with avoiding extremes of the left and right as we saw above. Today, and for many decades, the "problem" for the Business Roundtable is public opinion and the overall moral premise that capitalism is evil. As is fitting with their general approach, as described by Dr. Peikoff, pragmatists will only change the definition of the corporation and declare that the problem of public opinion is now solved (although they are really looking and seeing).

In other words, if the corporation was once meant to pursue **shareholder value**, holding *this* idea must be, according to pragmatists, a denial of the possibility of development and improvement. This old view of the corporation is the present problem with which they must deal. Yet, we must ask, how can holding to a specific definition be wrong if there is no reason to change it? Men are still doing business the way they always used to do. Their minds are still pursuing values in the way they always used to pursue; and the pricing mechanism still functions under the rules of supply and demand. So why change the definition of the corporation? To answer this question, remember the quote above: **"You have to try and see, you have to experiment, you have to see what works. You have to give up the idea of unyielding, unswerving loyalty to moral principles."** So, here you have it, pragmatism in action. Oh, but there is so much more.

If your previous concept of a corporation is no longer useful, if it is under attack, then the members of *this* organization solve the problem of today by putting a band aid on it. For them, the problem is threats from the government (antitrust, regulations, bad publicity, etc.) and a public opinion that views corporations as greedy and selfish. In fact, these illustrious CEOs make their million + salaries because they are trained on how to solve problems like bad public opinion.

They take a bold new leap by changing the definition of the corporation and including altruism within that definition. They make altruism the new social reality. But wait, that's not new. Remember what Dr. Peikoff said: They are merely making "a pronounced slant to the left"…as the country moves further to the left in general, the pragmatists are carried along."

In fact, many of the ideas coming out of the universities today involve a strong hatred of self-interest, capitalism and profits. Advocates of altruism (socialists, communists, fascists and pragmatists) excoriate CEOs for being selfish and predatory. The result is that CEOs who feel guilty for being "capitalists" often promise to give away their profits.

Indeed, the idea that the end (solving a problem) justifies the means (indoctrinating the shareholders) requires setting all opposition aside and forcing it to accept new altruistic trends and floating abstractions. This practice is a typical pragmatist tactic that has been used often by the left to politically disenfranchise free market advocates. No opposing argument stands a chance against the steamrolling of opinion as it is practiced by leftists in organizations such as the Business Roundtable. It is convenient for them that they routinely use altruism and the appeal to "doing good" in order to motivate society. The entire nation must now christen the new definition of the corporation and fall in line with the massive government-inspired giveaway of the profits of the corporation. Everything will be just fine if we all change our models of thinking.

If you doubt that Business Roundtable membership is made up of dupes for the politicians, consider these words: "those at the very top, the richest individuals and the richest corporations are going to pay more" (Warren), "we're going to stand up to the greed and corruption and price fixing of the pharmaceutical industries" (Sanders), "hell yes, we're going to take your AR-15s, your AK-47s" (O'Rourke), "I have proposed...that we, by 2028, cut all carbon emissions from new buildings, by 2030, carbon emissions from cars, and by 2035, all carbon emissions from the manufacture of electricity" (Warren), "as long as Washington is paying more attention to money than it is to our future, we can't make the changes we need to make. We have to attack the corruption head on" (Warren). Don't be surprised that most CEOs in this country agree with all of these statements. Don't be surprised that our government gets bigger and more oppressive every day. The pragmatists in the business world went to school with the pragmatists in government.

In the real world, a corporation is made up of departments, business units and managers that work cooperatively to achieve shareholder value. If any action within the corporation detracts from that goal, it is seen as counterproductive and harmful to shareholder value. Shareholders, seeing inefficiencies, would perceive the loss of value and take their investments elsewhere. This is called the movement of capital to better uses, a free market principle at the heart of capitalism. This hasn't changed. But the CEOs of the Business Roundtable want to change it – and for that they must rope the shareholders into christening the new definition of the corporation.

Many CEOs, educated as altruists since kindergarten, see the corporations' need for profits as selfish and they spend lots of money to produce well-polished press releases, prospectuses and earnings statements to convince shareholders that altruism and social responsibility are the best ways to earn profits. Like Leninists in the past, these rationalizations are intended to indoctrinate all parties that goodwill comes to the corporation through government contracts, subsidies and government grants, not to mention beneficial legislation that improves market share. By fostering the social goals of the government, the corporation declares itself a good community partner that puts people first not profits. How Dewey of them.

The CEOs of the Business Roundtable would likely respond to shareholder opposition by declaring that they should not be expected to buck the trend of the entire world toward corporate benevolence. Why should they have to take a stand against the trend of ever-growing government? One should not have to oppose a government that acts on behalf of all citizens by taking care of them, protecting their environment, making sure they have health care, childcare, free college and free everything. Why shouldn't citizens want to give up their guns now so that government can be their caretaker? All they are trying to do in the Business Roundtable is make sure they do their part. What is so bad about that? What kind of monster would oppose such benevolence?

As a young boy, I experienced the same guilt that today's CEOs experience. I was taught by parents and authority figures that I should never be selfish, and I should put other people first. I felt so guilty that I wondered how I could make my parents and peers love me. The answer was simple: I should put others first and sacrifice everything I had earned for others. If a young boy like me is horrified about thinking of himself first, don't be shocked then that even today's most well-educated executives feel they have to put others before profits.

These corporate strategies must work together without internal conflict. They must serve the interests of the shareholders who seek real bottom-line results. If a corporation declares that it will not seek profits alone, but also other goals not directly related to profits, the shareholders will take notice. This is because capitalism, real capitalism, depends upon **knowledge** (to make good business decisions) and **justice** to enable the best products and services to be created.

The Business Roundtable, on the other hand, is not made up of people who seek knowledge and justice. For them knowledge is not possible; their metaphysical principles don't recognize the existence of a means to knowledge nor even the possibility of it. As for justice, they prefer regulations that stifle their competitors. They don't want to win customers anymore; they want to capture them by making it impossible for the competition to flourish. This isn't capitalism but more like mercantilism, captive markets, government protectionism and conquered loot. This is loyalty marketing and the glues that hold it together are collectivism and altruism. Don't ask these CEOs to function in a free market – how could you? Free markets? That means greed and corruption just like Bernie Sanders said.

Many shareholders are "old-timers" like me. We think the result of seeking profits is an ever-improving society, a cleaner environment, better paid and happier employees and more efficient social institutions. For centuries, it was thought that the result of capitalism was our wonderful living environments, more leisure, better transportation, better highways, air conditioning and affluence for all citizens. The provision of jobs in a nurturing work environment meant happier, more productive, more intelligent and more dedicated employees; and this meant bigger markets for the products of the corporation. In short, capitalism has created many of the enjoyments of life and it lifts society by its constant development of value for the consumer. Profits are earned by the companies that do a better job of improving the lives of employees who are not downtrodden and poor but educated and affluent. The law of supply and demand and the free flow of capital are the hallmarks of capitalism; but not anymore. The successful company is the one who has a presence in DC, a company that "spreads the wealth" – the shareholders wealth.

What happened? Where did capitalism go? Why do CEOs think they need to re-define, not only the definition of the corporation but, as a consequence, the definition of capitalism itself? Where is capitalism failing that we have arrived at this situation? How is it that capitalism is blamed for creating the very poverty that it is lifting from society? There is no proof that capitalism is failing; there is only the pull to the left that Dr. Peikoff describes. Let's look at how they have re-defined the corporation.

They start with the following:

"Since 1978, Business Roundtable has periodically issued Principles of Corporate Governance. Each version of the document issued since 1997 has endorsed principles of shareholder primacy – **that corporations exist principally to serve shareholders.** With today's announcement, the new Statement supersedes previous statements and outlines a modern standard for corporate responsibility."[6] (Text bolded for emphasis)

"The American dream is alive, but fraying," said Jamie Dimon, Chairman and CEO of JPMorgan Chase & Co. and Chairman of Business Roundtable. "**Major employers are investing in their workers and communities because they know it is the only way to be successful over the long term. These modernized principles reflect the business community's unwavering commitment to continue to push for an economy that serves all Americans.**"[7] (Bolded text in the original)

Modernized principles? Is Mr. Dimon saying that American corporations have not invested in their employees and communities? I find it ludicrous that he says this since most of these companies hire only people with college degrees and they spend millions in training and supplementing employee knowledge. Most corporations have rigorous training programs and they reward good employees well.

Additionally, why does Mr. Dimon say that the American dream is fraying? One would think

6 https://www.businessroundtable.org/business-roundtable-redefines-the-purpose-of-a-corporation-to-promote-an-economy-that-serves-all-americans
7 Ibid

there is some sinister force causing this but there is no explanation found in this letter. I suggest that he and other CEOs are blind to what makes an economy flourish. They are blind to the role of knowledge and justice in a free economy because they are not operating in a free economy. As pragmatists, they gave up on that decades ago because of their woozy love of "democracy". Their talk about "modernized principles" means they foster, not freedom, but mercantilism, protectionism, regulation and monopoly power. I'd like to suggest a novel idea; the American dream is fraying because of massive government entitlement programs that divert corporate and taxpayer dollars away from production and toward "spending" which causes market distortions. In other words, the cause of our declining living standards is massive government spending and protectionist policies – this is what they call modernized principles.

But don't expect a corporation, eager to earn re-distributed money, to complain about ever-growing and ever-oppressive government. They don't want to anger their government benefactors. Corporate welfare is good for the bottom line. Their modernized principle is pragmatism that puts CEOs in a box with no choice but to promote the growth of government. Not only that, they must train their employees to accept the government line and to fervently believe in egalitarian principles. In other words, corporate executives must become progressives and so must all their employees. They must not question the goals of the government – in fact, they must enthusiastically mouth and repeat all the propaganda about "modernized principles". It is good for the company, they think.

Apparently, they are blind to the consequences of buying into the social justice mantra of progressive intellectuals. A whole nation of such progressives are destroying capitalism in favor of a collectivist democracy. The truth they ignore is that their policies and actions have led to economic depression, joblessness, corruption and monopolies protected by government. But, you see, they don't want to go to extremes. Let's just see how it works out.

The idea that the economy should serve all Americans must make you wonder. You cannot serve all Americans by spending your profits feeding the poor. Eventually, your profits dry up and there is nothing left to invest in the corporation. It is called diminishing returns. A good free market economist will tell you. But no one is asking.

"**"This new statement better reflects the way corporations can and should operate today**," added Alex Gorsky, Chairman of the Board and Chief Executive Officer of Johnson & Johnson and Chair of the Business Roundtable Corporate Governance Committee. "**It affirms the essential role corporations can play in improving our society when CEOs are truly committed to meeting the needs of all stakeholders**."

"Industry leaders also lent their support for the updated Business Roundtable Statement, citing the positive impact this commitment will have on long-term value creation:

"**"I welcome this thoughtful statement by Business Roundtable CEOs on the Purpose of a Corporation. By taking a broader, more complete view of corporate purpose, boards can focus on creating long-term value, better serving everyone – investors, employees, communities, suppliers and customers**," said Bill McNabb, former CEO of Vanguard."

"**"CEOs work to generate profits and return value to shareholders, but the best-run companies do more. They put the customer first** and invest in their employees and communities. In the end, it's the most promising way to build long-term value," said Tricia Griffith, President and CEO of Progressive Corporation.""[8]

"Statement on the Purpose of a Corporation

"Americans deserve an economy that allows each person to succeed through hard work and creativity and to lead a life of meaning and dignity. We believe the free-market system is the best means of generating good jobs, a strong and sustainable economy, innovation, a healthy environment and economic opportunity for all.

"Businesses play a vital role in the economy by creating jobs, fostering innovation and providing essential goods and services. Businesses make and sell consumer products; manufacture equipment and vehicles; support the national defense; grow and produce food; provide health care; generate and deliver energy; and offer financial, communications and other services that underpin economic growth.

"While each of our individual companies serves its own corporate purpose, we share a fundamental commitment to all of our stakeholders. We commit to:

---

[8] Ibid

- Delivering value to our customers. We will further the tradition of American companies leading the way in meeting or exceeding customer expectations.

- Investing in our employees. This starts with compensating them fairly and providing important benefits. It also includes supporting them through training and education that help develop new skills for a rapidly changing world. We foster diversity and inclusion, dignity and respect.

- Dealing fairly and ethically with our suppliers. We are dedicated to serving as good partners to the other companies, large and small, that help us meet our missions.

- Supporting the communities in which we work. We respect the people in our communities and protect the environment by embracing sustainable practices across our businesses.

- Generating long-term value for shareholders, who provide the capital that allows companies to invest, grow and innovate. We are committed to transparency and effective engagement with shareholders.

"Each of our stakeholders is essential. We commit to deliver value to all of them, for the future success of our companies, our communities and our country."[9] (Bolded text in the original)

How do we understand this monumental re-definition? Did they consult any epistemologists about this change in definitions? Did they back up their re-definition with scientific studies on how to increase profits through strategic investing or did they just pull it out of their kindergarten moral training?

Keep in mind that the statement, "we share a fundamental commitment to all of our stakeholders" is a drastic change from **"corporations exist principally to serve shareholders"**. How is it even possible for a group of powerful business executives to change a definition that has stood the test of time? They do it because they want to feed at the government trough.

To understand this, let's look at the modern corporation. One popular idea is called the business/government alliance. It calls for a "working relationship" between government and business for the sake of society. Keep in mind,

---

[9] Ibid

this alliance would not be deemed necessary if the government did not have such a massive hold (force) on our entire economy. In fact, the idea of this alliance has been used by corporate propagandists to highlight a company's willingness to cooperate with government and advance the wellbeing of society as a whole. Even Hillary Clinton had promised to work with corporations to improve the economy while she was running for President. By cooperating with government, businesses are seen as "smart" and practical. And the media is eager to promote the idea with lots of positive coverage. That it actually represents a rope around the necks of corporate CEOs is something everyone denies (nervously).

The CEOs of the Business Roundtable have convinced themselves they are practical men who know how to get things done. They are true pragmatists seeking creativity and democracy. They even praise themselves, and the politicians they work with, for their "modernized principles", forward thinking and intelligence. Who wouldn't want to work with the government responsible for "investing" so much taxpayer money in society?

But then deciding to work with government doesn't take a high IQ. Any chiseler knows that the best way to rob people is to join forces with the robber. In the past, we called gangsters what they were; and we refused to enable them. Today, we call gangsters enlightened politicians who love the people. My question is how could CEOs be so short-sighted? How could they have joined the gang? The answer is they too are muscling in on the tax-payer funding bonanza and they are justified because of the woozy socialism that is working its way through society.

I am not mincing words here; corporations working with government involves criminality and it goes to the question of how can those trained in the best colleges, groomed to become leaders by those colleges, actually become criminals? The answer is that they were groomed to steal by the philosophies they were educated to practice. Yes, in our present circumstance, it is socio-economic in nature, but not in the way many people think.

"There are many, many reasons why socio-economic groups may have, not a monopoly, but an oligopoly, on crime that have nothing to do with whether or not man has volition. One of the countless reasons could be if another group that runs newspapers and schools spends all their time telling the first group that they are helpless victims of depraved injustice and that the only way to get what's coming to them is to commit crimes; if you know which groups I'm talking about. If that is dinned into peoples' ears, there will certainly be a strong tendency for the recipient group to go out march and riot in the streets. That will not prove determinism but ideological corruption of their teachers. And the culprits therefore are not the socio-economic groups you have in mind, ... but the people who are teaching them that the solution to their problems is not work, effort and freedom, but government handout or outright murder. In other words, it is the volition of the New York Times and Harvard University that is the culprit here, not the non-volition of the socio-economic group in question. So even if the statistics were right and criminality was much more advanced among the poor or the black or the whichever, that would have nothing to do with volition, or with justice or with philosophy. It would only have to be the reflection on the corrupt philosophy of the people educating these groups."[10]

---

[10] Moral Virtue, a lecture by Dr. Leonard Peikoff

Certainly, then, the "teachers" from the elite universities are the very teachers who have been educating our CEOs. They have been teaching young people from this elite socio-economic group that it is proper and moral for them to seek every government handout they can obtain; and even more, it is their duty to turn their corporations into social service organizations that serve the very people who are being decimated by the brash pursuit of profit and advantage. The result of this corrupt ideology is criminality; a justification for every individual, poor and rich, to get what he or she can from government.

Today, business leaders proclaim a new social consciousness, a desire to work for the whole of humanity rather than mere profits and shareholder value. Let's look again at the Business Roundtable announcement.

- Delivering value to our customers. We will further the tradition of American companies leading the way in meeting or exceeding customer expectations.

  - **My comment: Actually, it is interesting that this particular focus on the customer is the means most corporations use in order to positively influence shareholder**

value. It seems this was listed first in order to lay a cover of respectability over the new priorities. What are they hiding?

- Investing in our employees. This starts with compensating them fairly and providing important benefits. It also includes supporting them through training and education that help develop new skills for a rapidly changing world. We foster diversity and inclusion, dignity and respect.

    - **My comment: If there is anything that American corporations do and have done throughout the history of capitalism is pay its employees better than other less-capitalist countries. Again, we have lip-service to a condition that already exists. What this *really* means is that corporations will adopt the minimum wage that will make government happy. So, they are appeasing government by raising wages and the cost of production which raises prices – not good for shareholder value.**

- Dealing fairly and ethically with our suppliers. We are dedicated to serving as good partners to the other companies, large and small, that help us meet our missions.

- **My comment: Again, this situation is largely already at a high level in our economy. It declares that corporations will now take on a new attitude and "sacrifice" their profits for the sake of companies that are already rich because of the large amounts of government business they do. This is lip-service again for a situation that already exists - but it might also signal an interest by Roundtable corporations to enrich themselves through supplier acquisitions. Clever, don't you think?**

- Supporting the communities in which we work. We respect the people in our communities and protect the environment by embracing sustainable practices across our businesses.

  - **My comment: Again, this is another signal to the government and, in particular, to the leftists who are insisting we stop fossil fuel usage and convert to less productive and more expensive sources of energy. These**

companies have committed to raising the cost of production by declaring environmental concern. But they must back it up by eliminating fossil fuel usage. Not good for shareholder value.

- Generating long-term value for shareholders, who provide the capital that allows companies to invest, grow and innovate. We are committed to transparency and effective engagement with shareholders.

  - **My comment: Finally, we have arrived at the old definition of the corporation, now relegated to last place. One assumes that the CEOs of the Business Roundtable are prepared to "indoctrinate" employees, communities and shareholders about their new responsibilities. Remember, the old communist line that once all citizens are living for the state, the society would be free of capitalism and the government would wither away? Don't count on it. Just as in the Soviet Union, such a goal destroys all**

capitalist principles, and this would destroy affluence and who knows how many people.

"Now the real work must begin. Moving from intention to action to indoctrination will require significant resources and a great deal of courageous patience."[11] Yes, you read that right. The mask has slipped, and the authoritarian state has shown its face in the corporation. In order to turn this new definition of the corporation into reality, they must spend vast amounts of money "indoctrinating" society to get on board. I'm sure the government will be glad to help.

The new definition of the corporation is nothing more than propaganda intended to convince people that today's profit-seeking corporations have changed their tune. And indeed, they have; they are no longer concerned with *themselves* but with *society*. The CEOs of these corporations, like good pragmatists, believe that perception is reality and they think their new focus on social responsibility will change society and cause

---

[11] https://www.linkedin.com/pulse/open-letter-ceos-business-roundtable-bob-chapman/

people to have a better *"perception"* of them. Their target is the public, consumers and shareholders who should all be properly indoctrinated into the value of community-oriented corporations.

Given this new perspective of the corporation, the public, it is hoped, will close its eyes to how much money the corporations will spend on "indoctrination". The employees will be diverted from production to "helping others" (and lose their careers in the process) while the shareholders will be happy to keep their money in the corporations. Other companies and consumers, seeing this new twist on profits, will be eager to trade with the corporations because of their new people-directed priorities. Everyone will be happy and modernized.

Yet, there is something hidden beneath all the indoctrination and love. The CEOs and management of these companies are now tools of the socialist state; their companies are soon to be looted of their value. And, what is worse; they are saying to the government looters: "Come and get us. We are ripe for destruction."

All this love and good will makes my head spin and I remember the words of one of my favorites, John Allison.

"There is a major philosophical trap based on the most common cultural beliefs in our society that undermines many business leaders. This trap is the combination of altruism and pragmatism... Altruism demands that our primary goal in life is to serve others. You cannot seriously be an altruist and run a successful business in a competitive market. Altruism demands that any time you develop a market advantage, you have to turn over the advantage to your competitors. One would soon be out of business if one were to take this approach seriously. Business leaders often pay lip service to altruism, but they know they cannot be an altruist in practice and still stay in business. However, because they believe they should be altruistic, business leaders experience guilt and conflict, sometimes leading them to make poor decisions and often depriving them of much earned happiness.

"This contradiction that businessmen find themselves trying to uphold is an illusion. Business is noble work. The noblest act of a businessman is creating better products and services and earning the wealth which comes from this process.

"It is very easy to give money away (especially if it isn't yours), but earning it is hard. Think of the irony and injustice that occurs whenever a business leader is told to "give back to the community" or face moral scorn—that business leader has already created a better standard of living for his customers and provided jobs for employees."[12]

Some might say that I am failing to understand the new Business Roundtable approach. I am seeing a sinister motive where there is only love and understanding. In other words, I am unable to understand that the new pragmatism of the Business Roundtable is **actually working**. There's that pragmatist slogan again. The world is changing. Why think in such negative terms about a positive development?

Pragmatism is based upon influencing the opinions of *people* rather than convincing them about value in the corporation. A corporation, under this principle, wins when it convinces people that it is working for *them* and not for profits. This implies that the corporation has always been the evil villain that anti-capitalist critics had claimed. Rather than deny evil intentions, the CEOs are basically saying that the vicious critics were right. They are, in effect, affirming the lie that capitalism is a system of

---

[12] Introduction to Why Businessmen Need Philosophy by Ayn Rand

exploitation rather than a system of value and free trade.

But what does capitulating to the haters of capitalism win for the corporations? All it wins is thoughts; not dollars. All it accomplishes is the spending of money on indoctrination. The real "practical" result of believing that perception is reality is the admission that capitalism is managed by guilty little boys with their hands in the cookie jar. The anti-capitalist will not say "thank you" and change his mind about the new corporatism. Instead, he will ask why the corporations should be allowed to make millions selling what they should be giving away? Isn't the next trend nationalization by the government? In fact, by acquiescing to the haters of capitalism, the giants of the Business Roundtable are smuggling unworkable and impractical ideas into the definition of the corporation.

To see this from a wider philosophical perspective let's look at the behavior of most major corporations today. We will see that they are not so "clean" and virtuous as they want to appear. When we do this, we will see that today's corporations are essentially *not* capitalist organizations anymore. They have lost their principles long ago, including the principle that the primary purpose of a corporation is shareholder value.

In accepting the propaganda of anti-capitalism, business executives are making themselves into tools of the government. Here is how:

- They foster the social goals of the government such as diversity, egalitarianism, political correctness, environmentalism and other goals. They do this because they think selling out will get business *from* the government. What they don't realize is that they are selling out to charlatans who will use the power given to them for their own financial gain – at the expense of the corporation. For instance, diversity training is an effort to indoctrinate employees to foster collectivism and groupthink. Environmentalism diverts companies from using the most efficient energy sources while enabling government control of the energy industry. Political correctness governs speech and silences opposing views which stifles creativity and innovation. All such measures stifle freedom within the corporation and in the marketplace.

- They spend billions every year on lobbyists to influence legislation and regulations. Much of this spending is pure bribery and waste because politicians have learned that the best way to skim corporate profits is to threaten takeover, regulation and antitrust prosecutions. On the legislative front, they pay for the chance to write their own regulations in order to give themselves an advantage over competitors. But there is a heavy price to pay for this "access" because this money comes from profits and it enriches corrupt politicians who know how to "play the game". I submit this is a perpetual "game" that leads eventually to collapse when all the money runs out. There is no magic bailout at the end of the road.
- They pursue government contracts worth billions in order to leverage their market position and make competing easier. This favors the corporations over smaller competitors who can't "play the game".

- They pursue subsidies and government grants while kick backs and stock options go to politicians.
- Despite the fact that the Citizens United Supreme Court decision confirmed their right to freedom of speech, they continue to support the government line on virtually every issue in order to signal to the government that they are "good citizens" worthy of preferential treatment.

These activities reveal the utter corruption of the business/government alliance. They have more to do with the failure of socialism than capitalism. What's more, they don't work in the long-term. In fact, playing with the government can land many corporate executives in prison as politicians double-cross them for the sake of votes.

Everyone knows that businesses today have a very bad press. So many voices in society are anti-business. Creating a new definition of the corporation is not the answer. Everyone knows that corporations are only about profits and this is proper. Everything the Business Roundtable does to convince people otherwise will fall flat.

Corporations will not be able to out-social-justice the social justice warriors, no matter how hard they try because the social justice warriors are not about social justice; they are about milking the corporations of money.

The truth is that corporations should not try to convince us they are moral. They should own up to the fact that capitalism has done more good than the social justice warriors by a long shot. They should not play the pragmatist game of destroying capitalism but should be spending their money supporting free markets. In fact, the corporations are already providing more value than the very social-justice warriors they are trying to appease. But no one knows it because the corporations are too busy capitulating to the very people who hate them.

I'd suggest that CEOs go back to putting profits first. They should stop collaborating with government looters and especially stop selling to government the rope they will use to hang them. There is no need for the corporations to "give back" to the people because they have stolen nothing from them. In fact, society is much better because we have had capitalism. Better to make great products and impress shareholders rather than to make social responsibility the highest value. Stop the bribery and virtue signalling.

The truth is the executives of the Business Roundtable no longer represent capitalism because they have been pursuing the business/government alliance and seeking to change the meaning of capitalism. The result is that they have been stagnating as producers and they are ripe to be surpassed by the next group of innovators. Their days are numbered. All it takes is a new idea hatched in someone's garage – not a new charity program.

If CEOs today want to get capitalism back, they must embrace capitalism openly and stop apologizing to people. They must stand for principles such as individual rights, laissez faire capitalism, the free flow of capital, the law of supply and demand and they should declare their rights. There is only one viable long-term strategy for the corporations today: they should be good at what they do, be innovative and competitive. Rather than caving-in to their enemies, they should fight those enemies and stop their advance toward totalitarianism. They should not buckle under to the shakedowns. They must fight the business/government alliance as a bad idea fraught with dangerous consequences such as the demise of liberty and capitalism. Their biggest enemy is in their own heads; it is the idea that collaborating with government is practical.

Where has the Business Roundtable been going wrong? They think they can turn concepts (like "the corporation") into their opposites. They think they can base corporate policies on buzzwords repeated over and over. Far from displaying their sophistication and intelligence, they expose their short-sightedness. Definitions only change when new knowledge is applied to them. They do not change when we apply a false moral philosophy, altruism, and pin its various characteristics to the corporation.

Unfortunately for the CEOs of the Business Roundtable, capitalism and altruism represent two opposite moral principles. I urge businesspeople to come home to the moral philosophy of capitalism which is egoism and self-interest. You can't save capitalism by becoming St. Francis of Assisi. You can't save society by smoothing over the real meaning of altruism (which is that egoism and self-interest must be destroyed). Compromising with a lethal enemy is the surest way to ensure you wind up serving the interests of that enemy. Do you think AOC and

Bernie Sanders are kidding about their intentions?

You cannot indoctrinate employees, customers and shareholders through diversity programs, social service projects, sustainability initiatives, charity and lobbying efforts, all of which divert much needed profits from shareholder earnings. If you are going to "inspire" people, why not inspire them to accomplishment, innovation, thinking out of the box, and creating new and better products? When you try to indoctrinate people into accepting new definitions, you only antagonize people who, most often, have a better sense of history and morality than you think.

The CEOs of the Business Roundtable are most likely not aware of the damage they are doing to society and, in particular, their customers. As pragmatists, they deny the nature of reality and put the onus of truth on a collective which has very little real power – most collectives fail. The end does not justify the means.

What's wrong with the corporation? It is the philosophy of pragmatism which countenances several false premises, not the least of which is the morality of self-sacrifice (altruism); the primacy of duty. Pragmatism defaults to altruism and collectivism as a matter or course.

Additionally, the idea that you can deal with reality by influencing the minds of men is a fool's errand. Existence exists independently of consciousness. Reality is not made by the opinions of men. To pursue the idea that society is made by the minds of men will not bring good results for corporations.

Capitalism is premised on reality and facts not on opinions. One obtains satisfied customers by providing tangible values. In this sense, yes, the customer is always right. Products and services can only be traded by men who associate with the best; the best minds, the best management techniques, the best products for men who want the best lives. It is not about indoctrination, nor is it about being an effective communicator of social policy. It is about offering the best to men in the form of tangible benefits. For that, the corporation needs science and reason, not moral compromise.

Pragmatism starts with the Humean model of thinking which essentially disintegrates the human mind by slicing reality into concrete "facts" without integrating those facts into usable knowledge. Hume even said that we could not see the connection between cause and effect so therefore it did not exist. What does this view do to a person's ability to learn, know and make conclusions?

The fact that the human mind is capable of reason — independently of the minds of others — is the key fact that should guide capitalists. Being concrete-bound, on the other hand, means being unable to integrate knowledge into wider abstractions, principles and facts. This leads to a denial of cause and effect (you can't see necessity) and to cognitive doubt — which leads to bold leaps into the ether. This is the mentality of most CEOs who have been educated in the "top" universities.

Pragmatists present themselves as intelligent problem solvers when they are actually blindly playing wack-a-mole to any problem that raises its head. In fact, they don't know what to do but take risks with our lives. They do not have the courage to disagree with the government because they have been taught they should "democratically" compromise with any strong statement made by anyone. They have never learned how to analyze issues and come up with comprehensive solutions based upon sound scientific analysis. They are pseudo-scientists grabbing whatever unsound idea happens to float by them. That's why they never solve problems and default toward altruism (re-distribution) as virtually their only solution.

The Business Roundtable is a case in point. Its effort to change the definition of the corporation is an example of pragmatists trying to solve the problem of a disapproving press. Their "solution" is to default to social justice by re-distributing their profits to the very people who disapprove of their profit motive.

All the protestations about their new social responsibility and community involvement have nothing to do with society or communities; they are only about solving the problem of their low public opinion. The shareholders should be wary of their money being siphoned off in this way.

The Business Roundtable's effort to change the definition of the corporation is impractical. It won't work; no one will buy the pretense of social consciousness regardless of how hard they try and how much money they waste on "indoctrination". Pragmatism, because it starts with an addled mind, is a weak philosophy countenancing compromise, force, fraud and government harassment of corporations.

To understand this, let's get to the fundamental nature of pragmatism – why it is impractical. W. T. Jones, in the quote I mentioned above said that pragmatists were influenced by "Kant's phenomena (but not his noumena)". This influence is critical to understanding why pragmatism cannot solve problems in the real world. What is the issue here?

First of all, Kant's metaphysics postulated two realms; the noumenal and the phenomenal. "In the simplest sense, Kant says that there are two different worlds. The first world is called the noumenal world. It is the world of things outside us, the world of things as they really are, the world of trees, dogs, cars, houses and fluff that are really real. However, Kant says, our minds are created in such a way that we cannot comprehend this world as it really is. Instead what we perceive is like an altered version of this world which Kant called the phenomenal world. The phenomenal world is the world that we perceive or to put it another way, the view we have of the world that is inside our heads...

"So why doesn't information come cleanly into our heads from out there in the real world? Why do things get messed up on the way in? Kant's answer is that a number of axioms, assumptions or rules (which he also called schema) are hard wired into our minds and they interact with the real (noumenal) world to help create the phenomenal world that exists inside our heads. In a sense these axioms or rules are like a filter between our minds and the real world, a bit like a man who is wearing sunglasses. The sunglasses are like the schema and they alter the way that the world really looks to create the world that exists inside our heads, as such the man with the sunglasses on will see things as blacker or darker than they really are."[13]

13
http://www.mrhoyestokwebsite.com/WOKs/Reason/Useful%20Information/Noumenal%20&%20Phenomenal.htm

The Objectivist—September 1971
Kant And Self-Sacrifice
By Leonard Peikoff

Real but unknowable   Not real, a distortion

> My comment: How can Kant or man even conceive of a real self if it is unknowable? Why doesn't he just deny that it exists since it can't be known? How did Kant know?

> My comment: No proof that man is divided in this way - how did Kant know it? If we can know only the phenomenal, how did he know the noumenal? What are the consequences of this division for human psychology and moral decision-making?

Man's unreal foot in the Phenomenal

> My comment: How did he know this, how did he validate it? How could man possibly know that one of the "feet" is un real? Is he trying to stand on two feet and is just incompetent or is the incompetent because neither foot is efficacious?

Man's real foot in the Noumenal - source of morality, the creator of duties, categorical imperatives demands unconditional obedience - human reason can't help here because se it is caught in the phenomenal in the world of appearances - man must obey them freely

Noumenal World
Unknowable - but man is the author in himself of these

Phenomenal World
Experience acquaints man with this

Kant's Divided Self

"Man is, therefore, a creature in metaphysical conflict, a dual creature— much more deeply so than the Enlightenment (or even the medieval era) imagined; he is, so to speak, a metaphysical biped, with one (unreal) foot in the phenomenal world, and one (unknowable) foot in the noumenal world." - Peikoff

"It is the noumenal foot that is the source of morality, the creator of man's duties, the entity which issues categorical imperatives to men and demands unconditional obedience. Kant calls it "a priori practical reason" (or "pure" will)— something entirely different from "the particular nature of human reason". Man's "human reason" is unable by itself to provide a basis for morality; man's earthly will is ruled by the law of the pursuit of happiness; but when, in thought, we "transport ourselves" into "an order of things altogether different", we recognize that man can be" subject to certain laws," yet "independent as a thing or a being in itself"; we recognize that man's true (a priori practical) reason is replete with moral commandments, that his true (pure) will, transcending appearance, is "autonomous" and "free" - free to acknowledge the supreme authority of those commandments ar to obey them.

Thus, man on earth is obligated to heed the categorical imperatives of morality; he is obligated, whatever the resistance of his desires, because he himself—himself in itself—is their author." -Peikoff

Kant11.png

Please note that Kant's explanation (as well as that in the object above) is essentially a metaphor, a verbal expression that indicates how the mind works but without the actual pinpointing of the physical parts of the brain that do the filtering of information. The phenomenal world is "like" a device of some type that filters knowledge but without anyone actually finding the device and showing how it works. In short, even this simplified version of Kant's view is nothing more than an opinion that has scarcely been verified, examined and/or proven. It is a fiction.

The Objectivist—September 1971
Kant And Self-Sacrifice
By Leonard Peikoff

Real but unknowable   Not real, a distortion

"A man's self, [Kant] maintains, like everything else, is a part of reality- it, too, is something in itself- and if reality is unknowable, then *so is a man's self.* A man is able, Kant concludes, to know only his phenomenal ego, his self as it appears to him (in introspection); he cannot know his noumenal ego, his self as it is in itself." – Peikoff

My comment: How can Kant or man even conceive of a real self if it is unknowable? Why doesn't he just deny that it exists since it can't be known? How did Kant know?

My comment: No proof that reality is divided in this way - how did Kant know it? If we can know only the phenomenal, how did he know the noumenal?

My comment: How did he know this, how did he validate it? Why wouldn't man just "experience" this self as his real self and just be wrong without knowing it? Did Kant just deduce all of this from his metaphysical premise? If so, what is the danger in such a deduction since induction can never find it?

man's self as it appears to him - in introspection

Phenomenal World
Experience acquaints man with this

man's self as it is in itself- unknowable

Noumenal World
Unknowable

Kant's Unknowable Self

Kant10.png

53

Let's understand that Kant's designation of these two "worlds" is a false alternative. Things don't get messed up on their way into our heads. Contrary to Hume, man starts with sensations, moves to perceptions and then to concepts; this is a perfectly competent way for man to find understanding so long as he is diligent in his definitions and logic. One has to ask Hume and Kant how they came to be the only people in history to know that man is incapable of knowing? Aren't they refuting their own statements by assuming the power to make them? How can they "know" that man is incapable of knowing?

The truth is that Kant, through his writing, effectively set men up for cognitive failure. He said that the noumenal world was real but unknowable and the phenomenal world was made up of categories (filters) that were part of the makeup of the mind. In effect, one world was unknowable and the other was built up in man's mind. This effectively cut man off from the real world and gave him no access to it.

Anyone who accepted Kant's false alternative was sabotaged and incapable of knowing. This left men mired in deduction from Kantian psychology (this is a serious default with terrible consequences for human life). No wonder pragmatists must take bold leaps. They have no way of identifying problems because Kant cut off their access to reality and knowledge. This conceptual gargantuan sets up all intellectuals and, in particular every businessman and woman who wants to learn how to run big companies. What they are taught is pragmatism which, because it was supposedly invented by hard-headed Americans, was supposed to help us deal with reality. But it is Kant's reality they have been taught – a reality that isn't real.

Don't be surprised then that CEOs today are pragmatists incapable of solving problems. They are educated people with no sense of the real – the closest they get to the real is pragmatism's focus on utilitarianism (the greater good) and bold leaps (we have to try something) and then analysis of results that leaves the status quo in place. It is only after they take their bold leaps that they look to see whether they worked. There is no prior certainty for them because there are no principles allowed into the pragmatist method.

One thing you can't help notice is, as Dr. Peikoff informed us, pragmatists tend toward the left and they always tend toward indoctrinating people to make them altruistic and collectivist because that is the dominant morality in society. They don't have the ability to challenge sacred cows because they can't venture out into the pasture of the real world. And, if you'll look closely, the solutions they come up with are always new versions of the same solutions (re-distribution, altruism, socialism, utilitarianism) that got us into those problems (Look at the New Green Deal which is a massive government takeover and re-distribution scheme). Yet, when they look at the results of their solutions (failure) the only new idea they come up with is to tweak laws and regulations and policy all of which leave the problems in place. Don't ask the Business Roundtable to challenge the idea of sacrifice for the greater good. It is in their DNA to be failed technocrats.

I am suggesting that pragmatism is impractical and it leads American businesses into a dead end (or should I say a trap that leads to slavery). Instead of creating hard-headed realists, the universities create wimps who are afraid to challenge bad ideas. Their favorite word is "compromise". They claim to be scientific, but the only thing they do is hold focus groups, take polls and then recommend the same old solutions (re-distribution, altruism, socialism and utilitarianism).

The truth is that Kant's noumenal and phenomenal "worlds" are not alternatives to each other. They are not two opposites. They are two principles seeking to invalidate the human mind from two separate, but not opposite, perspectives. The opposing perspective to Kantian "worlds" has barely been identified, but it involves an objective approach to human thinking.

The mind begins to connect to reality by implicitly accepting the idea that existence exists and reality is what it is. In fact, it is the responsibility of the mind to perceive and identify the facts of reality, to develop and use knowledge to identify a proper moral code based upon epistemological clarity and logical, science-like deliberation. With this approach, you do not end up with an imperative to duty but to an adherence to reason and truth. The human mind is the instrument for the development of objective truth. This is what made man successful throughout the millennia. It is in his DNA to understand reality. The man that Hume and Kant describe is incapable of survival. Someone should have recognized this and blown the whistle on their neutering of the mind.

It is the advocates of capitalism that should champion an approach to objective knowledge and morality. It is the advocates of capitalism that should resist the call for social responsibility and political compromise with the left. It is the advocates of capitalism that should defend the rights of man to think, to deliberate and to act upon valid, scientifically derived truth, not to acquiesce to the enemies of truth and freedom.

It is capitalism that brought the world mass production, Say's Law, the law of supply and demand, the principle of capital accumulation, advanced forms of the division of labor and the principles of value creation and trade. It is capitalism that brought scientific induction to the issue of survival and it is capitalism that American CEOs should defend – not socialism and collectivist enslavement.

The new spirit of social responsibility of American corporations will not bring the world the next great innovation that will revolutionize living in America. It will not bring the next energy products, communication products, entertainment products, nutrition improvements and medical advances. Only the profit motive and the conviction that freedom drives innovation. Why advance ideas that are ideologically connected to failed socialist systems when those ideas are at the heart of the effort to destroy freedom and affluence?

What is wrong with the corporation today? Pragmatism brings with it fear and compromise and the idea that public opinion is more important than truth, the idea that profit is less important than duty and sacrifice. It is time for CEOs to get courage and recognize that the corporation should be proud it makes money.

Yet, there is hope that the American businessperson will recover from the stigma of pragmatism and become a truly "American" businessperson again; a "no nonsense" leader that wants facts, truth and principles. By developing an objective approach to thinking, the businessperson can strengthen his ability to advance science, truth and values in his dealings. He can reject the Kantian mindset that has trapped him in mindlessness and compromise. It may take a strong effort but, in truth, pragmatism is a weak philosophy and, eventually, Americans will discover that it does not hold up against the joy possible to a person who loves honest work. Certainly, many of the CEOs in the

Business Roundtable are irredeemable. They have bought into the primacy of duty and are riding on the coattails of giants of industry who invented the economy they are fortunate enough to have inherited. There is still enough of the American spirit left among them and we may yet be saved from the steamroller of leftism and re-distribution. But saving us will require a few new giants to come onto the scene; people who reject Kant's "phenomenal" world and embrace things as they are and things as they could be.

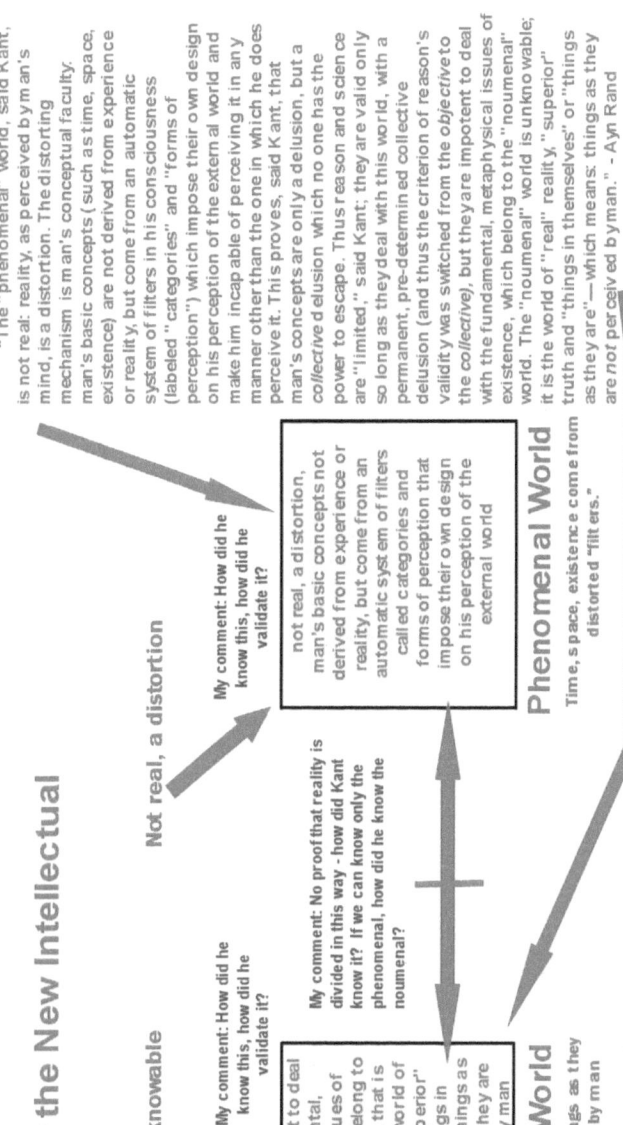

The Objectivist—September 1971

Kant And Self-Sacrifice

By Leonard Peikoff

My comment: Which is your real self? The Noumenal self is a package deal that replaces, not the phenomenal self but the real, integrated self of knowledge and reason with a false alternative that is a battle between the noumenal self as it fights off the emotional phenomenal self - a battle that is based upon a lie. The answer to this package deal is objective reality, reason and causality. - integration of all knowledge.

My comment: No proof that man is divided in this way - how did Kant know it? This is a false alternative that destroys lives through the confusion it engenders

"it is by reference to this concept of moral perfection - perfection as subjection to law in the absence of any love or desire, perfection as not merely disinterested but *uninterested* subjection to law, perfection as self-lessness, selflessness in the most profound and all-encompassing sense—that Kant evaluates man, and prescribes a code of action for him. Moral imperatives and duties, he states, exist only for a "will not absolutely good," i.e. for a *being with the capacity to hold personal values*. It is personal values that Kant condemns, not as evil, but as a "subjective imperfection" of man's lower, phenomenal nature- not as loathsome, but as meriting disdain and even "contempt," i.e. as unworthy of the distinctively *moral* emotion: respect. Full moral perfection, he believes, is impossible "to an earthly being who is subject to wants and inclinations..." Man is a "being not pure but tempted by desires" (and, therefore, "the moral law became known to mankind, as it must to any [such] being ... in the form of a *prohibition*"). I can approve a given inclination, declares Kant, but "I can have no respect for any inclination whatsoever, whether my own or that of another..." - Peikoff

man's lower nature meriting contempt - subjective imperfection

Phenomenal World
incapable of moral decision-making

moral perfection as subjection to law - to categorical imperative to self-sacrifice - condemn personal values - unworthy of respect or moral worth - do it because it is your duty - fight against desires

Noumenal World
categorical imperative

Kant's Moral Perfection

The Objectivist—September 1971
Kant And Self-Sacrifice
By Leonard Peikoff

My comment: For Kant, man is only perfect when he sacrifices and denies his own desires; but the sacrifice must be for the sake of sacrifice, not for the sake of being moral. Man must be at constant war against himself, denying himself with all of his effort. The answer to this package deal is objective reality, reason and causality. - integration of all knowledge. The best way to fully sacrifice all is to die, to deny all feeling.

My comment: No proof that man is divided in this way - how did Kant know it? This is a false alternative that destroys lives through the confusion it engenders

moral perfection as subjection to law - to categorical imperative to self-sacrifice - condemn personal values - unworthy of respect or moral worth - do it because it is your duty - fight against desires

Noumenal World
categorical imperative

man is imperfect and must experience desire for the things of this world - his wickedness is not that he desires but that he does not sacrifice his desires when duty demands - he can experience his desires to their fullest but must fight against them as well

Phenomenal World
incapable of moral decision-making

"The path to moral rebirth does not lie in the obliteration of self-love and its inclinations. Kant is not an ancient Stoic or a medieval ascetic or an Oriental mystic; he does not advocate the cessation of feeling. Man, he holds, is partly a phenomenal (and thus imperfect) being; as such, man must, *and should*, experience desire for the things of this world. Man's wickedness is not that he desires, but that he does not sacrifice his desires when duty demands it - not that he has needs and inclinations, "so impetuous" and "so plausible," (69) who se fulfillment "alone can make life worth desiring," but that he does not frustrate his needs, that he proceeds to *make* life worth desiring, i. e., to "cater to their satisfaction... in opposition to the law..." It is this which is "evil in itself, absolutely reprehensible, and must be completely eradicated..." Man's inclinations do present a certain problem: they "make difficult the *execution* of the good maxim which opposes them...."; but "genuine evil consists in this, that a man does not *will* to withstand those inclinations when they tempt him to transgress..." -Peikoff

Kant's Moral Rebirth - Give it all up

Kant14.png

Objectivism: The Philosophy of Ayn Rand
Chapter 11—Capitalism

Rousseau's Social Contract made more powerful by Kant

My comment: No proof for this

"noumenal" self in its self, an unknowable entity that imposes on men an austere life of duty. Kant insists; a man is obligated to do his duty because he *himself*—himself in itself—is the author of the duty.

Noumenal World
Source of duty

My comment: No proof that reality is divided in this way - how did Kant know it? If we can know only the phenomenal, how did he know the noumenal?

"phenomenal" self may be too superficial to understand that government force is really what his noumenal self in its self has imposed - duty is an end in itself

My comment: No proof for this

Phenomenal World
Incapable of understanding the wisdom of duty

"The statist replies that ... a [socialist government] monopoly is no threat to independence; government edicts are not force, he explains, because the people themselves, if it is a "people's republic" or a democracy, are the source of the government, which represents them. Tell it to the individual who is not represented by the government and does not agree with its plan for his life. Tell the kulak under Stalin, or the student in Tienamen Square, or the physician in Massachusetts that he is "really" the source of the laws (or tanks) being unleashed against him, appearances to the contrary notwithstanding. Historically, the modern root of this obscene notion is not, as is often said, Hegel, but his mentor, Kant. Kant postulated as man's essence a "noumenal" self, an unknowable entity that imposes on men an austere life of duty—but this is not an unjust imposition, Kant insists; a man is obligated to do his duty because he *himself*—himself in it self—is the author of the duty, even though his apparent or "phenomenal" self may be too superficial to understand this truth. Of course, only philosophers talk in such terms; politicians and journalists are content to cash in on the terms without mentioning them." - Peikoff

Kant's Morality - Slavery as Justice

Kant5.png

About Robert Villegas

Robert Villegas, Jr. is an Arizona Author specializing in fiction, romance, theater, religion, poetry, philosophy and business books. He was born in South Texas (Weslaco) but raised in Indiana. He is Hispanic-American but American in every sense of the word. He has spent a lifetime in the business world as a UPS executive and also worked in locations all over the United States and Europe. He is an Army veteran who served in Korea as a telecommunications specialist serving in the 7th Infantry Division in Camp Casey, Korea. He was educated in Indiana and earned a Degree through the University of the State of NY (Albany) via an external degree program. He is divorced with three grown children and three grandchildren. Famous relatives include Mexican anti-hero Dimas DeLeon and guitarist and music producer Johnny Garcia of Weslaco, TX (lead guitarist for Garth Brooks and Trisha Yearwood).

www.robertvillegas.com

To learn about Mr. Villegas' other books, check:

https://amzn.to/2ngaUHb

Alcoholism and Addiction – the System

These four books comprise a system that can be used by both patients and counselors who are battling Alcoholism and Addiction. Based upon Mr. Villegas's own system developed during his struggle against alcoholism, this system includes:

Alcoholism and Addiction – A Secular Ten-Step Program

This groundbreaking book offers a secular approach to alcoholism unlike that offered by Alcoholics Anonymous. We recommend that every individual going for alcohol and drug-abuse counseling be given a copy of this book which contains the workbook and the two versions of The World's first drunk. http://amzn.to/2md6R9w $3.45 Kindle $11.95 softcover

The Secular Ten-Step Program Workbook

This booklet covers the program developed by Mr. Villegas. It is designed as a workbook with blank spaces for the patient to write his own thoughts as he takes each of the ten steps. Order one copy for each patient in counseling. http://amzn.to/2lrHimS $4.49 Kindle $6.95 softcover

The World's First Drunk – With Counselor Talking Points

This booklet is designed for the counselor as he works with patients during individual or group therapy. It contains helpful tips on discussing the life story of the man who invented alcohol. Order one copy for each patient in counseling. http://amzn.to/2l446Wr $2.99 Kindle $5.95 softcover

The World's First Drunk – Patient Version

This version of the short story contains empty spaces where the patient can answer questions about the life story of the man who invented alcohol. Order one copy for each counselor. http://amzn.to/2ldxBGb $2.99 Kindle $5.95 softcover.

www.robertvillegas.com

Business Books by Robert Villegas

These four books by Robert Villegas comprise some of the business books that he has written. As an executive working for several companies, he was able to develop these methods that will help anyone seeking to excel in the business world. These books are:

How to Be a Great Employee – and a Greater Manager

You cannot be a great manager without first being a great employee. And this is something that requires learning, experience and attitude. The attitude comes from you but the learning and experience you should acquire through diligent study and practice. http://amzn.to/2BqdG2i $3.99 Kindle $8.95 softcover

SWOT Analysis Supercharged

A SWOT Analysis is an objective look at the internal and external elements of your organization that impact your success or lack thereof. If done diligently, you will always have a handle on what you need to do to improve season after season. http://amzn.to/2BCAWYx $3.99 Kindle $6.95 softcover

The Five-Module Call Center Training System

The Five-Module Call Center Training System is designed to assist the Call Center Team Leader in helping his employees quickly upgrade their skills to an acceptable level. http://amzn.to/2B3Svj1 $3.99 Kindle $5.95 softcover

Website Development Methodology

Effective strategic marketing requires the ability to differentiate the website development organization and its deliverables from those of the competition. http://amzn.to/2DnYMqh $2.99 Kindle $12.95 softcover.

www.robertvillegas.com

The REAL Purpose-Driven Life
After centuries of being told that it is not about you, it is time to set the record straight. You are a unique individual and your goal in life should be to achieve your own happiness.
https://amzn.to/2XyrpPf $3.50 Kindle $7.95 softcover

Values and Purpose Workbook
This book is about you. It's about time. After centuries of being told that nothing is about you, it is time to set the record straight. You are a unique individual and your goal in life should be to achieve your happiness. https://amzn.to/2XwlkTv $3.99 Kindle $8.95 softcover

www.robertvillegas.com

Christianity – A New Perspective on Jesus

These three books are based upon a new perspective on the life and person of Jesus. Based upon a new theory of the story of Jesus as an invention of the Roman Imperial Cult, these books add significant new evidence for this theory.

Unkilling Jesus

Starting with Atwill's Caesar's Messiah theories, this book explores the following questions. How was the story of Jesus's life written? Who was Paul and what was his role in the creation of Christianity? What was his provenance and did he actually meet the resurrected Christ? Who wrote Revelation and what was the document's purpose? Why was Domitian assassinated? Who was Clement and what was the nature of his relationships with Peter and Josephus? Were the Pseudo-Clementine materials really "pseudo"? Why did Saulus attack Justus? How were the gospels written? http://amzn.to/2itMCoO $3.99 Kindle $15.95 softcover

Domitian: The Final Messiah

The central goal of this book is to define the specific themes and concepts that make up Domitian's contribution to Christianity – in a sense, we are defining the specific Domitian overlay to the Christian materials originally developed for Titus. http://amzn.to/2yWMSlx $2.99 Kindle $6.95 softcover

Paul's Agon and the Mystification of History

Paul and Jesus are joined in one important way; the way of a miracle. They met on the road to Damascus while Paul supposedly pursued Christians. Jesus, in a sense, told Paul to get with the program and stop persecuting his people. In this incident, the Bible tells us that Jesus is already dead, and resurrected. This book argues otherwise. http://amzn.to/2zSDsuP $5.99 Kindle $19.95 softcover

www.robertvillegas.com